Ash Tree

GW00786420

By Sue Millard

ISBN: 978-0-9569469-8-0

Published by Prolebooks
www.prolebooks.co.uk

Remembering
Naomi Bernard
31 August 2005 - 15 July 2011

Cover photograph © Sue Millard

Sue Millard has written for many years. Her poetry has appeared, amongst other places, in Interpreter's House, Pennine Platform, Prole and Snakeskin. She writes widely about Fell ponies in respected journals and for the Fell Pony Society. In 2005, Hayloft published Sue's *Hoofprints in Eden*, an investigation of the background and recent history of fell ponies. She also has a teen novel, *Against The Odds,* published by J A Allen. Recently, Sue has started to explore different ways into print and electronic media through her own imprint, Jackdaw E Books, where she has four other titles available.

Foreword

There are some reactions in the experience of cancer which, it seems to me, are universal, and Sue Millard's moving poems for the loss of her granddaughter Naomi embrace them all. There is hope, often false, of a good outcome, detailed in the poem "Wild Strawberries" that 'spring will come/ and summer's fruits, and you shall have them all.'

And there is rage, as in the why me/why us? rage of "Godless": 'I've torn the god idea/ out of the smug blue sky, and I've murdered/ the devil too.'

The grace and sanguinity with which some cancer patients, and especially children, bear the cruelties of the disease and its treatments is salutary as in "Search bar" where Millard describes how Naomi drew thank-you notes 'for those who made your scars,/ took the year lightly.'

At some point comes the anguish of wanting the suffering to end, powerfully expressed in "A perfect way to go" where the poet wishes her docile horses would run wild and bear Naomi away 'in a gallop to the hills/…to cheat the miserable length of dying.'

Lastly comes a kind of consolation and resurrection, for life and love go on 'as if in death you touch the beauty that is life.'

All these mixed emotions are couched eloquently in the image of the ash tree which, rotten and old, had to be cut down, leaving a stump that Naomi loved to play on and which later puts out new growth that a new grandchild, a boy, tugs at as if pulling on the thread that binds the past to the present.

It has been a privilege to be asked to write this short foreword: Millard has expressed Naomi's story and her own feelings so strongly and so poignantly that I have felt deeply moved by this collection. I sincerely wish it and its publishers every success.

Gill McEvoy.   17.7.2013

Gill McEvoy is the author of the poetry collections *Rise* and *The Plucking Shed*, both available from Cinnamon Press.

Contents

Wild strawberries was first published in Prole Magazine Issue 1, May 2010
Godless was runner-up in Prolebooks' Prole Laureate competition, Autumn 2010
Wings was first published in Prole Magazine Issue 3, October 2010
False Prophets was broadcast twice on BBC Radio Cumbria, April 2011
Pink was first published in The Interpreter's House Issue 49, February 2012; and reprinted by Candlestick Press, June 2012
Ash tree was first published in Prole Magazine issue 7, May 2012

Wild strawberries

The strawberries are gone. Your nimble hands
seized them with glee when the shadowy side
was still green-white.
This year you've missed the best.

Next year—when hospitals and surgery
are only memories, confused with fun
and work at school, and spinning swings, and sun
sparkling off the river's rippled surface
a hop skip jump away—then you and I
shall sit on our garden steps, and watch the bees
bumble in and out of the wall. We'll pick
wild strawberries, and not disturb them.
Live
        through scareful time, this ominous autumn.

Weather the winter, and the spring will come,
and summer's fruits; and you shall have them all.

Search Bar

The search bar can stay empty.
I can face facts, but now
I don't have nerve to seek them.

You skipped down sterile corridors,
bore lead-lined rooms, and tubes,
drank black sleep when you had to,
came to and smiled;
drew thank-you pictures
for those who made your scars,
took the year lightly.

These shadows on the screen
threaten your victory.

I've walked too far
into details, stitching symptoms,
recalling ghost-frail family, all eyes,
now dead. Fear stings me when I read
the academic words, the few
per-cent who live two years.

I'll search no more.

False Prophets

Don't believe the blackbird.
He's precocious, starts to sing
false golden trails of promises
of love and nests and hatching
in New Year's twilight.

Never mind old cock-robin.
North wind or snow, his shout
and his puffed bright chest
are war, not love; "Get the hell out,
I'll keep my garden."

Don't trust the bald-faced rook.
Shaking wings, he croaks pretence
of song, but he's a fraud
with his blueblack iridescence,
postures and won't build.

But let the truth-teller sing
his moorish music; haunted flute
blown here on the southern gales.
The sober bird in the tweed suit,
the curlew is spring.

Godless

For Leslie, Ivan, and Tom
and for Naomi

There is no god in heaven. I'll believe
in anything but that puppetmaster,
that mercenary concert manager.
No-one's in charge. I've torn the god idea
out of its smug blue sky, and I've murdered
the devil too. We can't blame them for death
now, or thank them for life. We fight alone.
No-one need pray for us. They waste their breath.

We trust the call of blood, the bond of kin;
we scorn soft sentiment and sympathy.
A touch of hands, a day spent in the sun,
the doing of what's needed in due time,
these are our comfort and our sanity:
the solid shield of ordinary things.

Wings

A pipistrelle, caught by the cat with one
needle-clawed swipe in last night's hunting spree,
lies here uneaten - its thin chamois stretched
across fine finger bones, chewed to black lace.
You reach out softly: "Can we draw it, please?"
The marvellousness of a mouse that flies!

Helping you, I'm again the timid child
behind a schoolyard stack of broken desks
stroking a sparrow's beautiful dead wing.
I knew death would be unforgiving—cold
rain would spatter dirt and tag the feathers,
the body stink until the maggots crawl;
I itched to draw that flirting rustling
tiered array of primaries, to keep back
something from the dust, before the bullies
clawed it from my hand and shrieked disgust.
I wrenched those pretty feathers from the corpse,
hid them, then showed, with lies, my empty palms.

I teach you, now, watching through younger eyes
your pencil shape the outline of a wing.
Your hands quick in your work, your questioning
full of delight at capturing a fact,
you look me in the face un-shamed: as if
through death you touch the beauty that is life.

Catching Swallows

Last year, thousands of miles ago,
these birds were hatchlings here. Now parents
red bibbed and navy suited,
they fight the wet wind
twittering of speed and life.

Their chicks squat with tails outspread
and hurt, clownish mouths.
They can't yet flip their wings
to lift and live; their flutter
to the windowsill
is a Biscay crossing.
A cold gust whacks them earthwards.

When the light begins to fade
the woman picks the fledglings from her path.
Fragments of breathing feather,
their black-wire claws cling tight.
She moves to shelter
the mystery
that should fly to Africa, and hope.

Ariadne

You know the minotaur
lurks in your own heart,
brain, blood and lungs.

You don't want to go exploring
empty or not-so-empty rooms
where the lack of light
may not mean nobody's in.

There is no dark darker
than the dark inside you.

Take the knife, now.
Here's the thread
for your other hand.
Hold it tight.

Thirteenth

We lay awake last night
past twelve,
skin to skin,
hands clasped,
keeping vigil;
not giving in
to the thirteenth day.
Maybe a good thing
still might happen—
she may live
and love and marry—
never be
a woman grieving
for her child
and for her child.

Ash tree

Look there, that break. See, where the rot's exposed?
She's weak. If the next gale blows easterly
she'll be gone. Best fell her; lop off her limbs,
rip down her head and grey-ribbed trunk. Then crack
twigs into kindling, logs into billets,
chop out the rot. The rest can burn—smoke, shine,
sink, and crumble into ash—all follows
from the first clean-cut mercy of the saw.

It's different for you, child. We used knives
first, and then drugs and more knives in the hope
that love and games and laughter might survive.
We weep inside now, knowing that the rot
is swelling up to choke you. We can ask
no mercy like the saw we gave the ash.

Doses

They roll on the table
like so many bullets,
a rearguard amalgam,
no silver among them.
You sort them by taste,
metallic, sweet, bitter.
You name them by ear.
The Greek and the Latin
roll off your tongue,
naïve childish patter,
rocks in the cradle.
You suck them all in,
your shudder controlled,
your swallow precise,
in charge of the whole
for the moment. But soon,
they'll call for a back-up—
a slow-release patch
stuck on your shoulder,
just where you can't scratch.

Mini Rally

I can see you, high
on the stump of the old ash tree
waving jazz hands
at the Mini Rally passing,
and jazz hands waving back
over their steering wheels.
I failed to photograph
your bouncy spirit
but I still see you there.

A perfect way to go

You sit up in the sun and laugh—
embroidered trousers creeping up your knees,
the mare's broad back your confidence.

The gelding following to the gate
has no foreknowledge—doesn't see
the tumour squeezing shut your lung,
the bursts of terror as you cough,
your screwed-up morphine sucking face.

In one fierce ache
I wish my beasts would drop their care
and run wild. I would sling you on,
unhelmeted and happy. In a gallop to the hills
perhaps you'd find a swift and perfect death
to cheat the miserable length of dying.

Many waters

Silence the birds. Their notes drop
sweet as spring, but hope
is too stale for me to drink now.

Shut up the poems. I can only make
stars that splash into uncontrolled
wet angles, slashed across the white.

Dry up the rain. I can water
deserts with these tears, my face the shore,
each indrawn breath salt as the sea.

Hush the goodbyes. I shall watch
while your river flows to the falls,
and try to smile for you.

Missing

Requiescat Naomi
31 August 2005 – 15 July 2011

I missed you by a quarter of an hour.
I should have hurried through my morning shower,
missed eating breakfast in the sleepy sun
or read no emails, or replied to none.

I miss you from the house when I arrive—
everything silent that was once alive.
The nurses meet me at the stair. Their kind,
practised updating powerblasts my mind.

I miss you from that waxy, sleeplike face.
Your thin hands curl without their living grace.
It's you with self subtracted. And I wail
till my throat hurts me like a swallowed nail.

I'll miss your heart, the things forever not—
the family, the life you'd yet to plot,
the cure you'll never find—the future star
that cannot now outshine the one you are.

Pink

White horses still their clattering feet
and wait for you.
In shadow street their pink-plumed heads
stand straight for you.
The lady at the bus-stop signs
a cross for you,
the walker with the terrier dog
sighs loss for you;
the traffic at the roundabout
must queue for you;
the metronome of trotting hooves
beats true for you.
The wagons on the carriageway
change gears for you;
the rider on the cycle-path
wipes tears for you.
Pink rose-bay and foxgloves paint
July for you;
the sunlight on the fell pours down
goodbye for you.
The smiles of all who met you weave
the pall for you;
that pink box in a white hearse is
too small for you.
A sailing group of pink balloons
learn flight with you
and high the wings of wheeling birds
delight with you.

Putting away the toys

The furry fox and the dishevelled doll
are someone else's cute creation,
dead easy to pack up and store.
But crayoned pages, full
of lettering and sums, fall slithering
to spill remembered glee at being you.

Your fingers formed that flower, that tree,
always to give away, never for you.
Grandad and smiles and thank-you notes,
those are to keep. Drug-numb,
you staggered on. It's for the grit,
for the wide grin, my body weeps.

I hold the brightness of you here;
I can't slay shadows by forbidding light.
They've named a star for you
that glitters like the cards you made
with kisses, 'Love, Naomi.'

Avatar

The funny photo, the one
with your tongue stuck out and your fingers spread,
grins off a mug, and the one I took of you
asking Grandad to try on your sunglasses
waits on the sideboard by your moneybox.

Your drawing of us both, so wickedly observed,
was once my avatar, but I've been
your black-edged portrait since the day you died.

I wondered yesterday, when should I change
again? Perhaps it's now, when I can face that grin
from the last weeks you felt alive.

Over Night

There was a full moon last night.

Rising through trees, its round face
shone bright and idiot-calm,
as the same moon two years past
saw your long farewell begin.

I went to bed, and dreamed
I stood outside your house, in its tight
little-town street, and the door was shut
and the windows dark. Clouds hid the moon
and someone else
slept inside.

Rain wetted the street—not the wild
rain of the fell, that hisses on the wind
and smacks like surf—it touched
old roofs, new-painted walls, impartially,
cloth-soft and without passion.

When I woke, it had rained in truth—
sweetly cleansed all,
like a baptism.

Phoenix from the Ash

Even on old maps
her presence by the road
was marked with its own symbol.
Look at the scars
from the assaults she's borne
and the breadth of that sawn-off bole.
Look at her roots dug deep into the rock
and her twigs stoutly bursting back to life.

Next summer or the next,
the boy with his grandad's grin
will climb onto that broad stump,
his red-gold hair gleaming. While he tugs
at the leaves that spring from her black buds,
I'll tell him of his sister, how she loved him
though they would never meet, and how
she danced up there, in purple and in pink.

Other Prolebook publications
Full details at: www.prolebooks.co.uk

Wendy Pratt weaves the voice of the witch Nan Hardwicke through her own to explore love, grief, lust and loss. The poems, often hauntingly personal, centre around the loss of Wendy's stillborn daughter, interspersed with the fantasy figure 'Nan' as we share in the depths of grief and the burning of a goat in 'Nan Hardwicke Turns into a Hare'.

In Nan Hardwicke Turns into a Hare... poems about the loss of a child are counterpointed by a series of monologues by the famous witch of the title... This imaginative collusion with female magic is perhaps one way of assuaging the pain of loss. But running with the witches might be another way of describing the consolations of poetry itself.
Andrew McCulloch, TLS
This is a searingly genuine document about an enormity of nature.
Andrew Sclater, Other Poetry

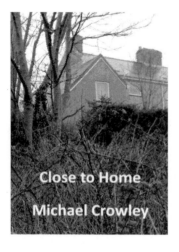

In his debut collection, *Close to Home*, poet and playwright, Michael Crowley, brings together three separate lives to create one existence in a collection that explores a displaced childhood, misplaced adults and the private moments that map a life.

Close to Home *shows Michael Crowley's ability to conjure place, character and emotion with no sentimentality but taking us right up to that edge so we are moved, delighted or, sometimes, horrified. The poems are lyrical and down-to-earth, urban with an understanding of how nature is a positive force in our lives.*
Alicia Stubbersfield